D0756346

45 4035503 4

Dinosaur!

by David Orme

Ransom

Trailblazers

Dinosaur!
by David Orme
Educational consultant: Helen Bird

Illustrated by Elisa Huber and Cyber Media (India) Ltd.

Published by Ransom Publishing Ltd.
Radley House, 8 St. Cross Road, Winchester, Hampshire, SO23 9HX, UK
www.ransom.co.uk

ISBN   978 184167 426 1

First published in 2006
Reprinted 2007, 2011

Copyright © 2006 Ransom Publishing Ltd.

Illustrations copyright © 2006 Elisa Huber and Ransom Publishing Ltd.

Thanks to Finn for the dinosaur footprint.

Every effort has been made to locate all copyright holders of material used in this book. If any errors or omissions have occurred, corrections will be made in future editions of this book.

A CIP catalogue record of this book is available from the British Library.

The rights of David Orme to be identified as the author and of Elisa Huber and Cyber Media (India) Ltd. to be identified as the illustrators of this Work have been asserted by them in accordance with sections 77 and 78 of the Copyright, Design and Patents Act 1988.

Dinosaur!

Contents

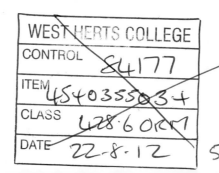

WEST HERTS COLLEGE

CONTROL 84177

ITEM 4540355034

CLASS 428.6 ORM

DATE 22-8-12   5.99

Dinosaur!

Get the facts

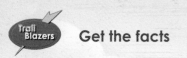
When did they live?

Millions of years ago the Earth was very different.

It was much hotter.

Most animals were dinosaurs.

6

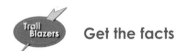
Killer dinosaurs

Some dinosaurs were meat eaters. They had huge teeth and claws.

These dinosaurs hunted and killed other dinosaurs.

T. Rex was a meat-eating dinosaur.

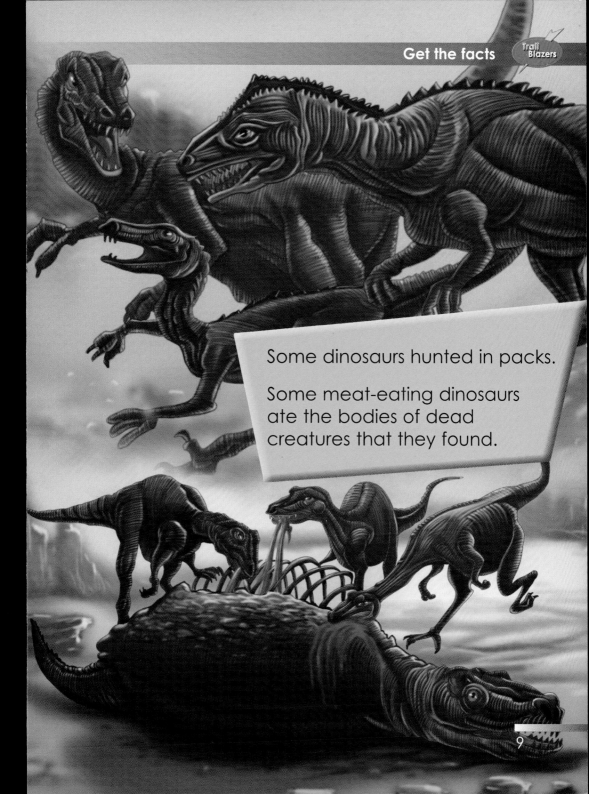

Some dinosaurs hunted in packs.

Some meat-eating dinosaurs ate the bodies of dead creatures that they found.

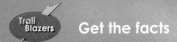
Giant dinosaurs

The biggest dinosaurs that ever lived were plant eaters. These dinosaurs grew so big because they had plenty of food.

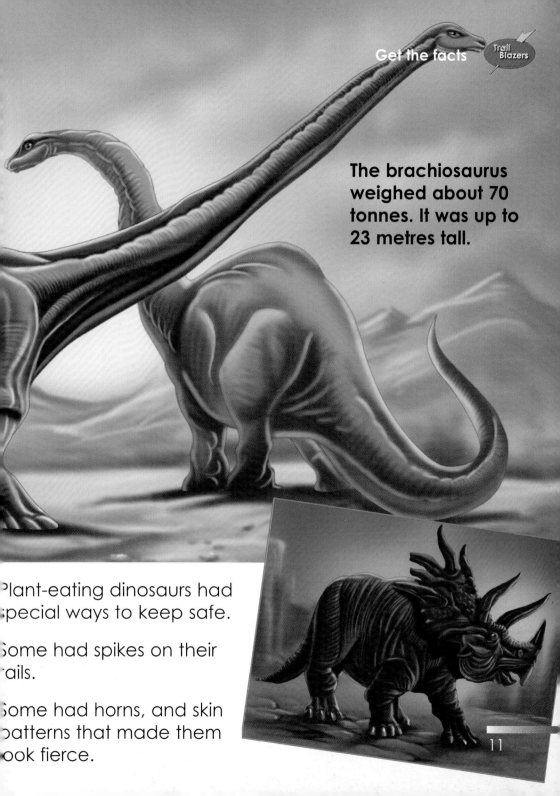

The brachiosaurus weighed about 70 tonnes. It was up to 23 metres tall.

Plant-eating dinosaurs had special ways to keep safe.

Some had spikes on their tails.

Some had horns, and skin patterns that made them look fierce.

11

The end of the dinosaurs

The dinosaurs were all killed off 65 million years ago.

People think a huge meteorite hit the Earth. It sent clouds of dust into the sky.

No sunlight could get through the dust and all the plants died.

The plant-eating dinosaurs died,
so the meat-eating dinosaurs
died too.

The only animals that lived
were in the sea or under
the ground.

Living dinosaurs

Some animals today may be related to dinosaurs.

Birds may have developed from flying dinosaurs.

Sharks lived in the sea at the time of the dinosaurs.

Many insects lived at the time of the dinosaurs. Most were like modern insects, though some were a lot bigger.

A fossil wasp

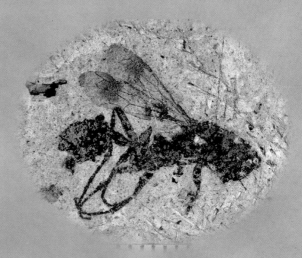

A modern wasp

Dinosaur hunting

Although there are no dinosaurs alive now, people like to find out about them.

There are dinosaur skeletons in museums.

People like to hunt for fossils.

Fossils are the remains of animals and plants that have made a pattern in the rocks.

You can find fossil dinosaur teeth, claws or bones.

Trail Blazers

You can even find fossil dinosaur footprints.

17

The Land Time Forgot

Chapter 1:
Dinosaur hunting

Terry and Julie were dinosaur hunters! The cliff near their home was full of fossils. They had found some amazing fossils. Their best one was a dinosaur footprint. It had been made in the mud over 65 million years ago.

Most of the fossils they found were not dinosaurs. They hoped one day they would find a dinosaur bone, maybe from a sort of dinosaur no-one had ever found before.

Terry and Julie were dinosaur hunters!

The best fossil they had ever found was a dinosaur footprint!

They didn't dig into the cliff. That could be dangerous. They looked for fossils on the beach. They hadn't found many today.

Terry was bending down, turning over stones. So Julie saw it first. Something amazing was happening.

"What's that mist?" she said. 'I've never seen green mist before! It's coming towards us along the beach!"

Something strange was happening on the beach . . .
Look! A green mist!
?!!

Chapter 2:
The green mist

It was a cold day, but warm air was coming from the mist.

"Look!" yelled Terry. "It's changing shape!"

"It's like a ring!" said Julie.

The mist in the middle of the ring cleared. They could see through it. Into another world!

"Look at those trees!" said Julie. "They look like trees from millions of years ago!"

"Move!" shouted Terry. "The ring is coming this way!"

The green misty ring came towards them faster than they could run. Suddenly Terry and Julie felt dizzy. For a moment, they couldn't see anything. When they stopped feeling dizzy the air was hot, and full of strange smells.

"Where are we?" said Julie.

The beach had disappeared. All around them was a strange jungle. And from the jungle came the roar of animals.

Chapter 3:
Pterodactyl attack

A terrible screech came from the sky. Terry and Julie looked up.

Terry gasped.

"It's a pterodactyl! But they've been extinct for millions of years!"

"That mist must have been a gate in time!" said Julie. "We've travelled into the past. Quick, let's get back to our own time!"

But the time gate had gone.

The pterodactyl swooped lower and lower.

"Quick, get under cover!" said Terry.

They ran into the trees. They hoped the pterodactyl wouldn't be able to attack them there. It was very swampy.

"These insects are horrible!" said Julie. "I'm getting bitten all over!"

"At least there's nothing bigger than insects here," said Terry.

Then they heard a roaring sound, and the crashing of trees.

Chapter 4:
He's missed us!

"That sounds really big!" said Julie. "We can't go into the open. The pterodactyl will get us!"

"We've got to. We can't run in this swamp!"

They rushed out of the trees. The pterodactyl had gone.

"Quick! Get behind these rocks!"

They were just in time!

"A T. Rex!" said Terry. "Looks like he's missed us!"

The huge creature crashed past them.

Suddenly the green mist came down.

They felt dizzy again. When the mist cleared they were back on the beach.

"That was amazing. But no one will believe us!" said Julie.

"I'm not sure about that," said Terry. "Look!"

Something else had come through the gate in time – the T. Rex!

The T. Rex had never eaten people before. But its journey from 65 million years ago had made it hungry. . . .

Dinosaur word check

amazing	insects
attack	jungle
believe	meteorite
brachiosaurus	millions
changing	modern
cleared	museums
creatures	packs
dangerous	patterns
developed	pterodactyl
different	remains
dinosaurs	roaring
disappeared	screech
dizzy	skeletons
dragonfly	sunlight
extinct	swampy
fierce	swooped
fossil	tonnes
horrible	weighed
hunted	